PATHFINDER: AN ACTION PLAN

MAKING THE MOST OF HIGH SCHOOL

FRANK C. LEANA, PHD
AND
CAROLE S. CLARK, MED

IUNIVERSE, INC.
NEW YORK   BLOOMINGTON

Pathfinder: An Action Plan
Making the Most of High School

iUniverse books may be ordered through booksellers or by contacting:

iUniverse
1663 Liberty Drive
Bloomington, IN 47403
www.iuniverse.com
1-800-Authors (1-800-288-4677)

Because of the dynamic nature of the Internet, any Web addresses or links contained in this book may have changed since publication and may no longer be valid.

ISBN: 978-1-4502-7015-1 (sc)
ISBN: 978-1-4502-7014-4 (ebk)

Library of Congress Control Number: 2010916854

Printed in the United States of America

iUniverse rev. date: 11/12/2010

For:

Elizabeth, Zachary, Eleanor, and Joseph
Elizabeth, Adam, Jackson, Morgan, and Wyatt
Jessica, Seiji, Emi, and Sumiko

CONTENTS

INTRODUCTION:
THE POWER OF CHOICE

Pathfinder: An Action Plan presents parents and children with a plan to work collaboratively to get the most out of high school. Students learn how to take charge of their choices, with the help of parents, guidance counselors, teachers, and advisors. The section "Hit the Road: The Journey" kicks off the plan. How students look back on their time in high school and how they feel those years have set them up for the next steps they take will ultimately be up to them. But one thing is certain: they will get more out of the experience and know themselves better if they play a meaningful role in the process.

Pathfinder: An Action Plan has the potential to be used as an aid to school counselors and psychologists and as a text in education classes. It explains how students can maximize what they get out of high school. Those who seek employment after high school will benefit from the planning presented to help develop interests, do as well as possible academically, and be proactive about learning.

Students from other countries looking to study in high schools in the United States or wanting to know what U.S. colleges expect from college applicants will profit from the general information contained in these pages and especially from knowing the specifics contained in the section "International Students Studying in the United States: Crossover."

One family said, as their son approached the college application process, "High school is not an ending—it is rather a commencement." Our hope is that, with proper planning, at graduation a self-realized, authentic individual will cross the stage to receive a diploma.

Students often feel that they have few choices in high school. Everyone has to take certain courses like math and English, as both are synonymous with success. Athletic prowess can determine social status and popularity. The day begins and ends at a set time, with bells and buzzers denoting moves from class to class. Reading the sections "Choosing Courses: Through a Class Darkly" and "Standardized Exams: Put to the Test," students might be surprised to see how much choice they actually have and how important these choices are. For those who are going on to college, this last step carries its own pressures. The final section, "What Matters Most to Colleges: The Next Step," addresses the relative importance of the various factors discussed throughout this book, such as course selection and leadership, used in the evaluation of an applicant's candidacy.

Choices made in high school have consequences. If they are aware of how one choice determines the next and leads to self-development and growth, students feel more in control of their lives than if they go passively through the motions, randomly choosing courses and haphazardly getting involved in extracurricular activities that lead nowhere and are ultimately unsatisfying. The section "Developing Interests and Activities: Sweating in the Dojo" addresses these issues and shows students how to take ownership of this part of their education. The sense of being invested in what happens day by day, year by year, for four years, is the best motivator for students to be players and not spectators in activities that lead to achievement and self-fulfillment.

Students who learn to take charge of their choices in high school make more impressive college or professional candidates because their character and sense of themselves as learners develop from within over time. Their profiles are not manufactured from the outside at the last minute to conform to a preconceived image.

In sports, it is virtually impossible to win consistently unless one understands the rules of the game. In the experience of high school, there are choices, attitudes, and behaviors that, similarly, determine whether the four years of high school add up to a win or a loss. The sections titled "Academic Solutions: Red Flags and Homework Hags" and "Learning Styles: Peeling the Label" discuss ways to increase academic achievement and address differences in learning styles to enable students to get all they can out of the academic experience. For some students, traditional high school is not the answer; "Alternatives to Traditional High School: Above and Beyond" presents alternatives. Students can learn how to work effectively with the authority figures in their lives; they can develop techniques, strategies, and behaviors—and sometimes alternatives—that allow them to understand what is expected of them.

We believe that *planning* and *preparation* trump *packaging*. Our aim in writing *Pathfinder: An Action Plan* is to give families and educators a clear understanding of how to help students make the journey through high school as meaningful as possible. The section "Table Talk: Parents Walk the Line" suggests how parents may take on a constructive role as guides for their sons and daughters. It contains practical advice, such as the importance of family dinners. We want the high school experience to be fun as well as fulfilling for both parents and students. That is most likely to happen when students enjoy learning because they understand why they are doing what they are doing and have played a part in that design, and when parents find positive and constructive ways to help. We want students to learn to navigate high school with direction, self-awareness, and joy.

HIT THE ROAD:
THE JOURNEY

"Did I call the right place? Do you do packaging?"

Was the caller looking for UPS or FedEx? Or perhaps a shipping company to specialty-wrap a precious work of art?

"Do you package kids? My son is really going to need packaging."

This father's precious work of art was his own son, a rising high school sophomore, looking ahead to the college application process. Something seemed wrong to us as counselors with this notion of a young person being viewed as a product in need of a sexy wrapping or pitch in order to be appealing to the college *market* or to prospective employers.

As the admission process to secondary schools and colleges, as well as competition for entry into the job force, become increasingly fierce, we hear the term *packaging* more often in our work as educational counselors. Although this anxious father's urgent question sounded blunt and misguided, the core of his concern reflected a trend. Parents were calling earlier in their students' secondary school years with specific concerns about high school. How would it influence college or career after graduation?

Had our father called the right office? Yes, because what he needed from us was not *packaging* but *planning*. Out of this father's sincere, if wrongly phrased, concern was born *Pathfinder: An Action Plan—Making the Most of High School*, a book to guide parents on how to work collaboratively with their sons and daughters to help them navigate the turns and detours of the adolescent passage through high school. If high school is viewed as a time of self-discovery and self-realization, choices and planning, then the notion of packaging becomes unnecessary.

The kind of thinking, which focuses on college placement rather than on the experience of high school, which can lead to college placement, is all too common. In our work as educational counselors, we try to help families frame the question differently.

We encourage families to think of the time between ninth and eleventh grades of high school as a journey that prepares the student for the eventual process of applying to college or for a job after senior year. Navigating the way through high school should be a thoughtful plan that is mindful of, but not fixated on, the ultimate destination, focusing instead on the steps along the way. Anyone who has been a member of AAA is familiar with the trademark *Triptik*®, a tool that breaks down a long journey into smaller segments. The driver using a *Triptik*® is alerted to detours, road conditions, highway speed traps, and other variables along the way, as she turns each page outlining a particular segment of the trip, mile by mile. The driver using the *Triptik®* knows that the ultimate destination is Cambridge but focuses on each milestone along the way, including tourist attractions and comfortable rest stops.

For the student in grades nine and ten, whether in day school or boarding school, the cornerstones are course selection, skill building, standardized testing, and the development of nonacademic interests and commitments. However, to continue the driving metaphor, the beginning high school student has only a learner's permit, not a full-fledged license. He/she cannot yet drive solo. Most of us can well remember how difficult it was for us to learn to drive with a parent in the passenger seat, exercising his or her critical judgment as we negotiated sharp turns and learned to shift gears. This is the time when communication and collaboration are paramount to the ultimate success of the process of getting ready to think about the college application process. Most ninth and tenth graders are not ready or willing to talk about applying to college, be it Harvard or the University of Michigan. So when parents jump-start the process and talk about what their children need to do to pave the way to a specific college, kids understandably become frightened and worry that they will not pass their road test. The typical ninth or tenth grader does not, and perhaps should not, have a clear destination yet. He or she should be urged to concentrate on getting the most out of high school and enjoying the ride. To do this, most students need help with problem-solving skills. It is the time when a driving instructor other than the parent can be so useful—a prized teacher, an educational consultant, a close relative, an advisor, or school counselor. Talking to ninth and tenth graders about concrete particulars such as course selection and commitment to a community service project is much more relevant and understandable—and much less threatening—to them, than talking about which college to attend or which job to seek.

There will always be obstacles in one's path and detours that call for a change of plans.

Understanding physics may prove impossible, and your best friend may be elected captain of the varsity lacrosse team instead of you. Thoughtful planning can help you to consider an alternate route that may, in fact, prove an advantage. For instance, deprived of the opportunity to be newspaper editor, one may explore a totally unfamiliar area and excel in it, becoming an outstanding debater.

We believe that getting the most out of high school includes self-discovery and self-realization. There are, indeed, road signs along the way. Students need to maximize the resources of high school as well as their own. For instance, they should follow a sequence of courses to the highest level at which they can do well, such as three lab sciences, or three years of foreign language. They should take risks and stretch their capabilities, for instance by trying out for a play or joining the debate team or writing for the school newspaper. It is important for one's own sense of self to develop an interest and take it to the top: try for a leadership role or an editorship or a captaincy. Then, when students actually begin the college exploration process midway through junior year, they will be equipped to start taking the wheel, to assume ownership of the process. The fusillade of standardized tests —PSAT, ACT, SAT I, SAT IIs, and AP exams— can be counterattacked by thoughtful planning that has occurred each year. SAT IIs can be spaced over time; for instance, biology SAT II at the end of grade nine and world history at the end of grade ten, rather than both being clumped together on one Saturday in June at the end of grade eleven. Students who have made the most of the high school experience, academically, socially, and personally, are ready to take charge of the college application process because they have been given the tools to do so. These are the college candidates who stand out in the applicant pool.

When it does become the right time to talk about college, if one has used the high school years to develop academic and extracurricular potential, then much of the groundwork has been established. One is not in the position of scurrying to make up for lost opportunity and time. It has been demonstrated time and again that students who maximize and enjoy the high school journey make more appealing and sought-after college candidates or employees.

When students are shown how to make informed choices about courses in high school, whether they head for college or a job, their background will be appropriate for the expectations that lie ahead. Such requirements cannot be met retroactively. Students interested in a career as a medical technician must study chemistry or biology. The student interested in business should have pursued math study. Exploring and developing their interests through joining clubs, actively committing to community service projects, or joining athletic teams enriches students' lives while creating character and confidence as well as building a résumé. There is no need to pad one's résumé at the last minute if the right moves have been made all along. Packaging is external; it is like window dressing, an artificial presentation. For instance, realizing during junior year that it would look good to a college or future employer to have engaged in community service, a student volunteers to work at a local home for the elderly. This is done merely to fill a blank on the activity section of an application or résumé, when prior to this, the student has shown little or no interest in this kind of outreach. By contrast, the student who plans develops this interest over time and might be heading toward a future in a helping profession.

What happens in thoughtful planning is that the commitment made becomes not only a part of what students do but of who they are. In packaging, the activity is merely a means of trying to look better on paper, with no integration into the personality. Whereas planning is evolutionary, packaging is an attempt at an instant fix. Learning how to study effectively, asking for help from teachers, seeking alternative styles of education, writing clearly, and speaking with conviction are lifelong strengths. These are just a few examples of how planning preempts packaging for either career or college. The question we would like parents to ask is, "Can you help us as a family understand how our son or daughter can get the most out of high school?" Whatever college or career eventually becomes the destination, the journey starts here.

CHOOSING COURSES :
THROUGH A CLASS DARKLY

A *course* is a way or a path, in addition to being a subject such as English, history, or math. The choice made sets one on a course of study that leads to understanding, insight, and future goals.

Courses that students choose help to determine both their academic path through four years of high school and the next journey, from high school to career or college. If more work is done in math and science than in the humanities such as English, art, and government, that decision may eventually lead toward higher study or a career in medicine or engineering rather than one in journalism or politics. On the other hand, there is much to be said for learning for learning's sake, for the joy of learning that many students experience by experimenting with a course in art history even while focusing on math or science. Discovery through a particular course in unfamiliar territory can take a student off one planned course and onto another, just as an unplanned exploration down a side street can take a visitor into an unexpected and delightful part of a new city.

I remember enjoying Latin in high school for three years, never asking why I was studying the ablative absolute. Our revered Latin teacher was fond of saying, "A dead language, huh? Well, what do people think when they see an omnibus coming down the street?" oblivious to the fact that no one actually referred to city buses as omnibuses anymore. Later, when I began to prepare for the SAT and was studying prefixes and suffixes, I saw how relevant Latin was to the study of English vocabulary. I was also learning how to study any foreign language, which helped me begin French in college. In graduate school, the required History of the English Language course made a lot more sense because I knew Latin. Students frequently complain about having to study a foreign language or calculus when they see no practical use for them. Although relevance is not always readily apparent, it often becomes clear later on. And we adults need to encourage students to experience the delight that lies in discovery as they explore new fields of learning. There is satisfaction in learning that takes us to new heights of thought and understanding, whether we are studying the development of the human figure from cave painting through Picasso or the patterns that are evident in history from colonial through postmodern periods. Following sequences, becoming aware of interdisciplinary connections, and experimentation on a canvas or in the lab are all very important as students are guided through course selection.

At the time of filling out college applications, students will be asked what they want to major in. It is important at that time to be credible by having done well. In other words, it is unwise to choose science if one's grades in that are or have been less than impressive. One launches oneself into the application process by bouncing off proven strengths.

Choosing courses is not, therefore, based on an absolute set of *musts*. Highly selective colleges do have certain expectations, but as we discussed above, there is room for some individual selection amidst those expectations. Choices need to be made based on the individual student's sense of a larger plan with a reason behind it.

, MATH

A representative math sequence would include algebra, geometry, precalculus or trigonometry, and calculus. This sequence would put a student on the path to applying to a competitive college.

A student less gifted in pure math, or one interested in social science, such as sociology or psychology, might consider statistics and probability in lieu of calculus, or in addition. In some high schools, business math and accounting are offered under a math curriculum for students on a track into further business study, but these courses are not typically recognized as fulfilling a math sequence by selective colleges. Calculus is practically a must on that track. Even some colleges that have no distribution requirements and do not care if a student ever takes math expect that the student, before enrolling, will have studied calculus.

These decisions can only be made year-by-year as grades in math accrue. Unless students earn at least a B in precalculus, most high schools will not let them enter calculus. The student who has a more or less clear idea of a career path is at an advantage here over the liberal arts student with an undeclared major, in that the choice of business math over calculus or probability/statistics might make a lot of sense. Most students, since they do not have a clearly set career path, should think about studying math at least through precalculus or trig. Three years of high school math is a typical expectation of four-year colleges.

If you are thinking about a career in math, engineering, premed, research, or architecture, take as many courses in math and science as possible, following sequences to high levels—for instance, advanced placement physics after physics. Applicants to specialized schools such as Cal Tech, Clarkson, or MIT will have taken a rigorous curriculum in these areas and demonstrated the ability to do well in them. They are also likely to follow up high grades with high scores on the standardized tests, SAT II or AP, in these disciplines. Advanced Placement calculus AB is usually the highest-level math expected by even the most selective colleges. Advanced Placement calculus BC and above is designed to challenge the truly talented in math. Unless a student is considering premed, architecture, engineering, or a career such as astrophysics, and is a whiz at math, calculus AB should suffice.

The question arises of whether to elect math at the Honors, Advanced, or AP level, if offered, and perhaps get a lower grade or to take regular sections and get an A. Several years ago parents used to ask an illustrious dean of admission at a well-known West Coast university this question at information sessions and college nights. He answered, "Students who come to our university take the

AP course *and* get A's!" The students in these advanced sections are highly motivated and usually gifted in that subject area; one swims with the sharks in entering those waters. On the other hand, there is little to be gained by piling on advanced level courses and getting mediocre grades. *The key is balance.* Select a reasonable schedule that contains courses in areas of demonstrated academic strength and do well in them.

For young people thinking about entering business-related areas after high school, facility with numbers is essential, as are computer and word-processing skills. Entry-level positions in business also call for the ability to file, write coherent memos, and participate actively in regularly scheduled department or staff meetings. Students contemplating work in business immediately after high school might consider adding to their schedules courses in statistics, business math, accounting, writing, and public speaking. Broad exposure to business-related disciplines is smart preparation to meet opportunities that arise unexpectedly. Being well-informed and flexible provides an excellent chance to step up to the plate.

' SCIENCE

The most common sequence for the sciences includes biology, chemistry, and physics. After these three basic courses, a student with a particular interest in science can choose to accelerate in one or two of these fields by electing an AP course in junior or senior year. It is important that these courses be accompanied by a lab. Labs provide experiential learning, highly valued by premed, science research, health profession, and medical technology majors.

If a student does not want to continue at an AP level in science but wants to attend a top-tier school, it is smart for that student to choose a half-year science elective in senior year, such as astronomy, anatomy, marine biology, or environmental science rather than to carry no science on a schedule. Students who double up on a modern and classical language often cannot fit a fourth year of science into their schedules. That is understandable if they are going to emphasize language, arts, history, or English, for instance, and present themselves that way to colleges. It is important that there be a rationale for the choices being made. If a student knows early on that he or she will likely continue study in environmental science, then, of course, choosing ecology or marine biology over a basic physics course makes sense.

At many high schools, psychology is offered within the science department; if so, it can qualify as a fourth year of science. At other high schools, psychology is housed in the history or social science department, in which case it is not strictly speaking a science elective. Still, for students heading into education, sociology, psychology, social work, personnel work, or even law, the choice of psychology makes at least as much sense as studying advanced chemistry.

FOREIGN LANGUAGE

Most colleges that require foreign language study expect either two years each of two languages or three or four years of one. Some students like to do two years of a classical language and two of a modern one. Students who want to pursue two languages, each to a high level, usually have to sacrifice some high-level study in math or science in senior year, as discussed above, because schedules cannot accommodate all these courses at once. As we said earlier, that choice is sensible so long as there is a reason behind it. When colleges expect proficiency in a foreign language, that usually assumes study of at least three years in high school, in order to prove proficiency by taking either an SAT II, an AP exam, or the college's own privately administered proficiency test upon enrolling. If students do not perform up to the expected level of proficiency, which varies by college, they generally need to take the language once in college until they pass the exam. Some colleges allow students to fulfill a foreign language requirement by studying American Sign Language or courses in the literature, culture, and history of a country. It is important for students who are not good at foreign languages or unable to study foreign language because of a learning difference to know that variations like this exist, so they do not feel trapped by this requirement.

At many colleges a classicist is as sought after for admission as a first boat rower or cellist. Because many parents do not think study of classical languages is practical or translatable into earning power, these departments are underutilized, so someone with demonstrated interest and ability in the classics might get a boost in the admissions process if he or she is applying with the serious intention of further study in this area at the college level.

In an increasingly global society, the ability to communicate with clients in their first language is a valued skill. So often, we see signs in stores and banks advertising service in Spanish, Chinese, Japanese, or French, among other languages. Increasingly, students opt to study one classical and one modern language or two modern languages, one of them being Chinese or Japanese. Students heading into careers in international business and finance are well advised to include Chinese, Arabic, or Japanese. Latin and German remain basic to premed study; French, Spanish, Italian, Russian, and German are useful accompaniments to the study of literature, comparative literature, history, and art history.

′ English and History

Most English curricula are fairly set until senior year, at which time students have a choice among electives, such as Witchcraft in Literature, Women's Studies, and the Journey in Literature. The question in the area of English is whether or not to study at the Advanced or AP levels, if possible. If a student envisions a major in English or a career in writing, journalism, teaching, or communications, then by all means he or she should advance to the highest level at which he or she can perform well. Some students are better readers than writers, or vice versa, but an English major involves both sets of skills. If it is possible to take one of the AP exams in either English literature or composition, do so, or take the English literature SAT II.

The ability to write clear, grammatically correct, and cohesive memos and reports is highly prized by employers. In addition, courses in high school or activities such as debate club, which build confident, effective public-speaking abilities are invaluable and serve a student lifelong.

After history courses have introduced the student to ancient history (usually in middle school), American history and government, and European history, then the student can often choose interesting electives from among topics such as America in the 60s, Latin American history, China, or contemporary issues. Students interested in English or history should think about extending that interest beyond the classroom by working on the newspaper or literary magazine or by being involved in debate, Model UN, or student government.

⟩ ARTS

Students with talent should follow through in their studies to the point where they can assemble an impressive portfolio. Many college art departments specify what they want included, such as two life drawings, one three-dimension piece, one charcoal drawing, and one oil painting. This is a prerequisite if applying to an art school. If art is an interest within a liberal arts curriculum, then a student may want to back up that interest by submitting a portfolio to demonstrate the level of accomplishment she has reached. Many high schools have an arts requirement, which can be fulfilled by electing courses in studio art, music, drama, or courses such as ceramics, jewelry making, and filmmaking. These electives give students an opportunity to discover hidden talents and interests. They are fun and provide an alternative to textbook learning.

Actors and musicians are more likely to encounter auditions when they apply for roles or to colleges as theater majors or music majors, and they definitely will if applying to a conservatory. Students interested in demonstrating acting or musical talent often include a brief tape or CD highlighting their performances.

The Importance of Follow-through for Entrance to Highly Selective Colleges

Keep in mind that for those students interested in going on to college, the ability to take an interest to a high level of development and achievement is highly valued by college admissions because it is viewed as a promising trait in taking a college major to a high level of critical thinking, writing, or performance.

Whatever subject area is of most interest, students need to be helped to get involved using related skills in context. If they like to write, they should write for a school publication. If politics are of interest, they ought to join Model UN or a political campaign inside or outside of school. Science students should consider extra research in a lab or clinic or enter a science competition like Intel. Math students should consider Math Club or math contests. For more on this, see the section on developing interests, but for now, suffice it to say that an interest can develop into a passion if a student reaches beyond textbooks and classroom walls and takes it into a larger live-action arena.

For Those Choosing Not to Follow a Four-Year College-Prep Curriculum

Some students may well choose not to follow a college-prep curriculum. If so, there is more room for nonacademic electives, such as auto mechanics, ceramics, jewelry making, or wood or metal shop, or for science electives that do not carry lab credit. For students pursuing a path toward a job immediately after high school, it is important to refine word-processing and computer skills. In fact, this is a necessary skill for anyone, given our technologically oriented society.

Students heading toward a two-year associate's degree after high school need to research the requirements within their field of interest, such as dental assistant or veterinary assistant. Specialized areas such as these require science study. Areas such as hospitality management or recreational management carry the expectation that the student will have used vacation or after-school time to gain some experience in the area. Preprofessional study is highly likely to include work experience during the high school years.

In Summary

If a student is uncertain of his or her path after high school, then following a basic academic curriculum as outlined provides the security of keeping possibilities open. If a schedule is not filled with AP and lab courses, there is room to include electives of particular relevance to a career such as accounting, bookkeeping, or metal shop.

Each student should feel comfortable putting together the curriculum best suited to his or her interests and long-term goals and one that is directed toward his or her strengths as they emerge. It is important to keep in mind, however, that highly selective colleges do have specific requirements or expectations if an applicant is to be competitive in their pool. One cannot fulfill those requirements retroactively, which is why it is so important to understand the implications of course choices for college admission or job placement.

The conundrum is that most high school freshmen and sophomores have not yet identified their ambitions and interests fully, if at all. Yet certain pathways lead to certain choices later on, or curtail them. That is why we urge parents to encourage their children to strike a balance when choosing courses—a balance that keeps in mind the student's abilities and possible objectives so that choices are not unknowingly cut off. Set a course with an awareness of expectations beyond high school while also allowing for academic success and personal growth.

Standardized Exams:
Put to the Test

˒ PSAT

Most students will take the Preliminary Scholastic Aptitude Test in the early fall of their junior year on one of two days, depending upon the high school. Registration occurs at the time of the test, which is given in school and proctored by school administrators or faculty. There is no preregistration. Based on the results of this test, students may be considered Commended or National Merit Semifinalist candidates, to be announced in the fall of senior year based on state percentiles. If a semifinalist rises to finalist standing after submitting an essay and transcript, scholarship offers could be forthcoming.

Many schools offer the PSAT (PLAN) in the tenth grade as a practice run. If your school does not offer this trial test, a neighboring school that does may be willing to allow you to take it with their students. The PSAT scores are not sent to colleges, so there is no downside to taking it in the tenth grade for practice. These results provide an early indicator of a student's starting point on standardized tests of this type. Many tenth-grade students may not have covered the requisite math to solve every problem, but overall the results can be useful in determining how much test prep is advisable before taking the PSAT in eleventh grade. SAT I Math includes high-level math skills, algebra and functions, geometry, statistics, probability, and data analysis. If the scores in critical reading, math, and writing are high, students may want to postpone coaching for the SAT until getting back results from the junior year PSAT. If the scores are low, beginning preparation after the tenth-grade PSAT gives more lead time for gradual improvement rather than last-minute cramming.

, SAT I

Most juniors take the SAT I on one of two spring test dates, although some feel ready to approach it in the winter of junior year. If the SAT I is taken in winter or early spring, and the student requests the test booklet and answer sheet from ETS at a nominal fee, he or she can learn from mistakes. If further prep is called for, theoretically one could retake the SAT I in May or June of junior year and complete the basic standardized test requirement before senior year. This facilitates planning which colleges to visit over the summer. If, however, the scores fall below expectation, based on diagnostic tests, a student is well advised to wait until the fall of senior year before retaking the SAT I, using the intervening summer break to prepare.

Beginning in March of 2009, the Educational Testing Service allows students to select those SAT I and SAT II scores that they wish to send to colleges. Most colleges give students the benefit of taking the higher scores from each section of multiple administrations. Some colleges will average them. Therefore, if a student believes that by retaking the test she can raise her scores in at least one section, then it is useful to do so. Several highly selective colleges, however, require full disclosure. Students should check the specific requirements on each college Web site.

᛫ SAT IIs

Students should choose SAT IIs carefully and thoughtfully and focus on those on which they are likely to do well, based on experience in class and on diagnostic tests.

What does *do well* mean, exactly? For a selective college it means a score in the high 600s or 700s. Scores in the low- to mid-600s are healthy but not stunning. They don't make much of a difference in admission to selective colleges. In highly competitive fields such as engineering and premed, it makes sense to show only very high scores in science and math. Many specialized programs in health, science, and math do require very high scores for the applicant to be considered seriously, so if diagnostic testing is not encouraging, and the student has done well in these subjects in school, then serious test prep seems the only solution. Prep courses are available online: for example, from College Board at https://satonlinecourse. collegeboard.com.

SAT II subject tests are offered in the following disciplines: English literature; U.S. history; world history;

math Level 2; biology; chemistry; physics; languages for reading—French, German, modern Hebrew, Italian, Latin, and Spanish; languages for reading and listening—Chinese, French, German, Japanese, Korean, and Spanish; and the English Language Proficiency Test.

It is important to think about which of these tests students should take as they go through high school. The ideal time to take an SAT II is when one has just completed the course in that subject. Therefore, most students take an SAT II in June. With foreign languages, three years of language study is usually the best preparation to do well.

If a student completes biology in grade nine, the student and his/her parents should talk to the teacher of that course to determine whether the curriculum has been geared to prepare students for the SAT II test in that subject, since not all high school courses are. If a student has done well in the course, it may make sense to purchase a review book and do some extra preparation. The College Board publishes a book of actual SAT II tests from the recent past. Some families prefer to hire a tutor who specializes in that subject to provide extra preparation on material not covered in class or to help with review. Keep in mind that this is quite expensive. *Refer to the section on Academic Solutions.*

Some selective colleges expect that applicants will have at least two strong SAT IIs to send with their applications. Several require three. As a senior, a prospective applicant wants to be in the position of having the prerequisite qualifications to apply anywhere of interest, so planning ahead and taking SAT IIs over time where a high score can be predicted makes good sense.

· ACT

The alternative to the SAT I, the American College Test or ACT, gives students the option to submit or not submit the results from a particular administration. Therefore, one could take the ACT twice and choose which set of scores to submit. The ACT is similar to the SAT I but contains a section of reading comprehension based on scientific reasoning. These reflect a student's ability to problem-solve within the area of natural science rather than his or her knowledge of factual information.

There is also a writing section on the ACT that is optional; one chooses to register with it included or not. Now that there is no longer an SAT II in English writing, colleges tend to want to see a writing section from either the SAT I or the ACT. Some colleges, however, do not require or recommend this section, so if writing is a weak area, a student would have the choice to include it on the ACT, whereas it is a mandatory section on the SAT I.

Does coaching for standardized tests make sense? There is no question in our minds, based on many years of watching this phenomenon, that the conscientious and committed effort to improve scores usually does. This is due largely to a combination of the student's becoming more familiar with the test format, building confidence, increasing control over pacing, and building up endurance for a four-hour test, and, of course, learning test-taking strategies to save time and eliminate more obvious incorrect answers. It is also critical that students complete practice tests in between sessions with a tutor. Tutoring sessions alone do not seem to have as large an impact on raising scores as tutoring sessions combined with consistent attention to practice exercises between sessions. There are, of course, exceptions—for instance, when a student has a certifiable learning difference that affects processing speed or causes him or her to mis-mark the bubbles on the answer sheet. But even students who fit that description will want to do everything they can to improve their scores. It is impossible to be absolutely certain what difference tutoring for standardized tests will make. The proof lies only in the end result. Parents should go over the results of these tests carefully with teachers and school administrators to get an early read on their children's test-taking capabilities. If students have changed schools, they may have sat for the Secondary School Admission Test (SSAT), the Independent School Entrance Exam (ISEE), or an exam for a selective public or parochial school. Many schools administer standardized exams such as the Stanford Achievement Test or the Comprehensive Testing Program (CTP) on a regular basis to check on students' progress. These exams provide useful exposure to the format, as well as the endurance required, to approach this type of test effectively. They build critical thinking skills and reinforce test-taking ability.

A low SAT I or ACT score does not mean there is no right college on the horizon. Fortunately, many colleges do not require either test or any other standardized exams. One can contact the FairTest Web site for a complete list, but among those schools that do not require standardized tests are: Bard, Bates, Bowdoin, Dickinson, Holy Cross, Mt. Holyoke, Muhlenberg, Sarah Lawrence, and Wheaton (in Massachusetts).

Often, when the SAT I or ACT is not required, colleges do ask the student to submit an essay done for class with a grade and teacher comments, so it is important to keep samples from eleventh grade or the first half of twelfth.

Many states have their own examinations in specific subjects. Since the results of these exams are recorded on students' transcripts, they need to be approached with preparation. In courses that terminate with such an exam, the curriculum is usually set to meet the requirements of the test. But each student will have to assess his/her own individual needs for further preparation.

For students not considering college immediately after high school, the Department of Labor provides a Web site, CareerVoyages, with information on careers, training, and job search. It also contains subcategories such as "The Quickest Route to a Six-Figure Job." Individual states provide their own career planning sites—e.g., Florida offers free advice at www.FACTS.org, with tools to determine appropriate career choices to explore.

DEVELOPING INTERESTS
AND ACTIVITIES:
SWEATING IN THE DOJO

Asked what they do in their spare time, a majority of students reply, "What spare time?" In recent years, it has been something of a cliché to say that students need to develop a passion to stand out as candidates for college admission. And so we have seen students sent off on $4,000 trips to Third World countries to construct school wings, pave village roads, and build houses—all worthwhile activities but ones that, in most cases, have no connection to the student's past or current interests. I am skeptical that colleges are taken in by this attempt to construct or pad a dossier with activities that come out of nowhere. It is much more fulfilling and productive to build a résumé that grows out of, and builds on, interests than to construct one that is a patch job at the last minute to fill in gaps in an application's activity grid. Most of all, activities should be enjoyable as well as productive.

When thinking about which activities to pursue in high school, the rule of thumb is to demonstrate

- **consistency**—stick with them over time;

- **follow-through**—try to have the activity stem from a curricular interest or hobby; for instance, someone interested in classics might decide to join an archaeological dig over the summer or tutor younger students in Latin;

- **creativity**—be willing to take a risk and try something new.

Here are some ways that students can both enrich their high school experience and at the same time begin to build a profile that will serve them in the college or job application process.

ꞌ PORTFOLIO

Students interested in art should collect samples of their work over time with the ultimate objective of forming a portfolio to submit with applications. If applying to an art college such as the Rhode Island School of Design, the Fashion Institute of Technology, or the Savannah College of Art and Design, the student will be required to submit a portfolio. The specifications for these art-school portfolios are carefully defined and might include a sample of three-dimensional work, oil, acrylic, pencil, life drawing, etc. If a student is merely showing a liberal arts college that art or photography is an interest that they have developed to an impressive level of accomplishment, there are usually no specific requirements of what must be in that portfolio. A student would simply choose his or her best work. Students who intend to claim art as a major interest in college or pursue it as a career should take advantage of any opportunity to exhibit their work in local or school shows and submit entries to the school literary magazine, for example. It is important to take one's artwork beyond the studio.

Students who are writers may choose to assemble a writing portfolio of their best work. This might include a variety of kinds of writing—poetry, short stories, journalism, science fiction, research papers, or personal writing—or it might focus on one genre.

Quite a few colleges, especially those that do not require that the student submit standardized test scores, require a sample of writing with teacher comments and a grade, so it is important to save writing samples and make copies of them before sending them out. Usually the college specifies that it does not want a research paper or a piece of creative writing but rather a critical or analytical essay.

Students interested in music can consider submitting a CD of a performance; this should be no more than ten or fifteen minutes in length and should demonstrate versatility as well as talent. For instance, a vocalist might do one classical song and one show tune. Students who compose music might consider submitting a score. These submissions are usually directed to the appropriate instructor in the music department of the college, not to Admissions, unless a special art supplemental form is supplied with the application instructing the applicant to send it to Admissions.

Acting students should not submit an entire video or DVD of their role in the school musical. Instead, a collage of highlights is recommended. If acting is a main interest and the student is applying as a drama major, an audition is certain to be part of the application process, making a CD superfluous. It is important for acting students to have a drama coach, within school or without, who can help them choose and perfect their audition pieces.

˒ SUMMER COURSES

Summer courses are a means of demonstrating a high level of interest in a subject area. These are offered at boarding schools, day schools, and on many college campuses across the country and internationally. I am not talking about remedial work, but rather electing to take a course to develop one's knowledge further, prove one's ability to succeed at the college level, or take a course not offered at most high schools, such as neurobiology. Some students like to use the summer to develop their fluency in a foreign language, through immersion with a native family or by using that language to tutor children for whom it is a first language in another subject, such as English.

Work taken for college credit can be submitted with applications to colleges by providing a formal transcript of the course taken and the grade received. It is important, therefore, to save all contact information from such programs so that a transcript can be requested later.

˒ LEADERSHIP

It is rewarding to discover one's own leadership capacity. There are many clubs, organizations, elected student government positions, and mentoring opportunities that allow this quality to emerge. Working one's way up the ladder in a club, sport, or student government to a position of responsibility can be very satisfying as well as important later on in the college application process. It is impressive and meaningful to be chosen by faculty or peers to be captain of a sport, a dorm monitor, or a disciplinary committee member because it shows others' trust and confidence in the student as a solid citizen in the school community.

One excellent way to demonstrate leadership in school is to help get a new club or organization going where none exists. For instance, a student interested in culinary arts might want to form a food club and get classmates to sample ethnic cuisines; students have founded food drives, clothing drives, and events to raise money for charities. The list of possibilities is endless. Working with school administrators on all the bureaucratic and legal issues involved in forming an activity can be a worthwhile experience in and of itself, one that later might provide strong material for a college essay.

COMMUNITY SERVICE

Students struggle over this expectation more than many others, partly because they resent feeling "forced" to do good works through community service or volunteer work. They would rather the urge came from within. And yet these activities often surprise by how satisfying and rewarding they are and how much they teach us about ourselves. Obligation quickly turns to opportunity when a young child looks up at a student volunteer and says, "I looked forward all week to seeing you." One can discover a new part of his/her personality through doing community service, finding a purpose beyond one's personal needs in the needs of others, be they senior citizens, underprivileged children, recuperating patients, the blind, or an elderly uncle.

Developing interests and engaging consistently in activities are not about creating a résumé; that is only the after-effect. Being involved is about self-discovery, about finding new outlets for personal expression, about making a difference outside of school and classroom. By engaging in activities, one gathers experience that makes one more complete, more interesting, and a deeper person, with an awareness of the world beyond self and high school.

' TRAVEL

Travel expands the imagination, provides a deeper appreciation of cultural differences, and may, for the student interested in architecture and art, inform about classical or modern styles. It also offers the opportunity for photography, improving fluency in a language, journal writing, or drawing, among many other things.

Simply listing the many places one has traveled because a family has the means to do so counts for nothing, however, in the college application process. Expensive jaunts filled with luxury hotels and gourmet food with no connection to local people merely attest to privilege. They do not demonstrate any particular challenge undertaken, like scaling a mountain or bicycling over local terrain, or insights reached during the process.

What does make an impression is trips during which one lives with a local family or participates in the improvements of a village's roadways or hospital, such as the program American Farm School Academy, in which students live in a Greek village and participate in the daily life of that community.

Also important is building foreign language fluency by actually speaking the language. Many programs exist, sponsored by the American Field Service and various boarding schools, such as Phillips Andover or Choate, that are open to qualified students from other schools. There are also private companies like Where There Be Dragons that specialize in a specific area of the world, such as Asia. For a complete listing of such programs, consult an index such as *Peterson's Guide to Summer Activities for Teenagers* or *The Princeton Review Guide to Summer Opportunities*.

Students should maximize travel opportunities by keeping a journal, composing a portfolio of photographs, focusing on some aspect of the locale, such as architecture, people, children, landscape, or animals, or by drawing or painting. In other words, go beyond merely being a tourist. These extensions of the trip will come in handy as students write college essays or search to recall details of an experience before an interview.

, JOBS AND INTERNSHIPS

Parents will be happy to hear, no doubt, that instead of spending a lot of money for a summer program they should feel comfortable encouraging their older high school student to think about applying for a job for the summer after eleventh grade. It is often difficult to land a paying job because of age and the demand for such slots, but family friends and connections can be helpful with this effort. Colleges seem to respond positively to a student rolling up her/his sleeves and taking on a real job. Many students have no choice but to do this after school and on weekends in order to have spending money. Balancing a part-time job with schoolwork shows maturity and developed time management skills. It is beneficial when these jobs are in line with a student's longer-term career interests, such as work in a law office, investment firm, or hotel, but, as a complete break from school, many students prefer a summer job totally different from what they do all year, such as flipping hamburgers at a local diner, pumping gas, or selling T-shirts in a mall. None of these choices is a wrong one. It is all about what a student makes of the experience, what he/she learns from it.

Internships are usually not paid but can provide invaluable experience within a field such as publishing, health care, veterinary science, law, banking, or lab research. Sampling a field of interest, in other words, to build experience or just to test the waters of that potential career is beneficial.

SPORTS

Getting involved in a sport often leads to increased confidence personally and socially, a sense of camaraderie, an experience pushing oneself past current limitations to succeed for the team. It can engender qualities of leadership that may lead to a captaincy by eleventh or twelfth grade. Employers like to see that a student can play an effective role in a group.

The question is often asked whether it is necessary to be good at a sport, or at least involved in one, to be considered a strong college applicant. The answer is somewhat complicated. Most students are unlikely to be recruited athletes. For most high school students, sports are fun; they build character and team player-ship, and they provide important and healthy outlets for pent-up energy. Participation shows a capacity for ensemble work with a team, discipline, and the ability to balance the demands of a sport with schoolwork. Students who do not enjoy team sports should not feel obligated to participate in order to get into college. Martial arts, yoga, fitness exercise, modern dance, and solo sports such as ice skating are perfectly acceptable alternatives. What remains important is the ability to commit to an activity, stick with it over time, and do one's personal best.

Athletic ability developed to a level of national or regional recognition or ranking might well interest a college coach. College athletics are organized into Division I, II, and III. It is important to consult an index and the appropriate high school coach to determine at what level one might play a college sport. Naturally, Division I is extremely competitive. Athletes who train at camps over the summer are often observed by college coaches. There are levels within the divisions as well, so that one might qualify for lower Division I but not upper Division I. Students who intend to launch themselves into the college application process as potential athletic recruits should keep clips of star turns on the field or the court to be compiled into a short video.

Some students who are natural athletes are excellent at two or three varsity sports by senior year. This is very impressive, especially when combined with an excellent and demanding academic record, because it represents a rare achievement. Students often ask whether it is okay by senior year to give up one of these sports or "Will it look bad to colleges?" The academic record is far more important in the end than whether a student has played one or two or three sports at varsity level. If, with the added pressure of filling out applications and keeping up grades, participating in more than one team sport becomes burdensome, students should discuss this choice carefully with parents and advisors. A sport in itself is unlikely to get a student admitted without appropriate academic credentials, except in a very few instances, for exceptionally talented players.

› RÉSUMÉ

Whether a student is applying to a college or for a job after high school, his or her choices of academics, activities, and interests during the prior four years constitute a résumé. For the non-college-bound, extracurricular activities, in addition to providing enjoyment, channels for social development, and vehicles for self-development, are also important résumé-builders. Employers are interested in a job applicant's sense of civic duty, leadership, evidence of commitment and follow-through, and willingness to reach out beyond the self to address the needs of others. For the college-bound, résumés provide a platform for exhibiting talents and the advantages of being a good citizen as well as a good student.

Résumé formats may vary, but the content is crucial in distinguishing applicants. The résumé reveals the student's unique set of experiences as well as his or her potential contribution to the community. Increasingly, employers are seeking résumés of high school graduate job seekers and internship applicants that include GPAs. Maintaining good grades is therefore a priority not just for the college-bound student. *See Sample Student Résumé in Appendix.*

Points to remember in designing a student résumé:

- Do not pad your résumé with more activities than it is humanly possible to participate in over a given time.

- List only those activities relevant to the high school years. Grade school does not count unless the activities are continued.

- Be sure to indicate a desire to continue a particular activity beyond high school.

- Be accurate about titles, names of clubs or organizations, and dates.

- Do not list as a job an internship that was not a paid position even though it is a work experience. Be sure to differentiate between paid and volunteer/internship positions.

- Awards are accomplishments. Be sure to list them.

Often high school students are stymied by the thought of composing a résumé. Putting their lives on paper, whether in an activity grid or a job application, is overwhelming. This is a time when parents can remind their student of the value of time well spent. Those walks to raise money for charit*y are* significant!

INTERVIEW SKILLS

The acquisition of interview skills starts at an early age with simple questions and answers between children and their parents. For example, a toddler begins to understand the Q and A mode when asked, "Which of your books would you like to have read to you at bedtime?" By the time students are graduating from high school, however, college or job interviewers expect them to be poised, honest, thoughtful, informed, and self-revealing. Some students show an innate ability and ease at interviews; many more will require practice or training. Joining the high school debate team is an example of an opportunity to develop oral skills beyond the elementary Q and A and to develop a sense of confidence on the podium and off. *See Appendix for Sample Interview Questions.*

IN SUMMARY

Colleges and employers are not so much looking to spot excellence in a number of activities. They are more concerned to see that a student can be involved and take an interest to the top.

It is important to show throughout high school, especially in the last two years, that a student has learned to balance responsibilities. Not every student will have the time or opportunity to be involved in extracurricular activities with the same degree of commitment. The student who must work part-time or take a role in watching younger siblings cannot devote as much time to after-school clubs and sports. Balancing responsibilities effectively in high school is viewed by colleges and prospective employers as an important skill because college schedules are more flexible than high school schedules. Students must become their own time managers, knowing how much time to allot for the big paper due Thursday on *War and Peace* before the big game on Friday afternoon. Planning ahead is essential.

Frank C. Leana, PhD, and Carole S. Clark, MEd

Colleges vet a student's profile very carefully to determine whether he or she has shown the ability to keep up with a demanding workload while taking part in the life of the school or meeting outside commitments.

Academic Solutions: Red Flags and Homework Hags

One of our clients said to me, "I am tired of being a homework hag." I had heard of *helicopter parents*, but this ugly image of parent as hounding hag was new to me. She had always overseen her son's homework, which, as he grew older, incited arguments and resistance to school. Although he could not responsibly and adequately attend to his school responsibilities without help and intervention, this young man was struggling for independence from Mom at a critical developmental stage that made help from home feel humiliating.

It is the rare parent who can serve as an effective homework helper or supervisor beyond middle school. Emerging adolescents tend to experience parental help with homework and assignments as intrusive, emasculating, and very threatening to their growing need for independence. What used to be accepted as helpful support and concern is viewed as control. Parents who have successfully assisted their child up to this point find it difficult to accept that the rules are changing, however, and they often take it personally.

It is also difficult for parents to be objective and professional in the role of tutor or coach during the high school years. The temptation is strong to take over the assignment, to write the paragraph or crack the math problem, rather than showing the student how to do it. Anecdotes abound of the wounded egos of parents who have taken a heavy-handed role in an assignment that is returned by the teacher with a C+.

Where parents can continue to be helpful is by providing a quiet space set aside for study, free from the distractions of cell phones, video games, television, and computer chat rooms. Students need a well-lit place to do homework apart from the noise of normal family life. Some students study effectively to music, so that should be an individual choice. An appreciation of the value of learning and academic achievement is something that students absorb from the atmosphere of their home and the habits of their parents.

ASKING FOR HELP

It is sometimes very difficult for teens and adolescents to admit the need for help and to understand how to go about asking for it if they do.

Teens often view the need for academic help as a sign of weakness. Boys can be especially self-conscious about this need. I used to remind my high school classes that if they don't understand information being presented by the teacher, chances are many other students are not grasping it, either. If asking a question in class feels too awkward, students need to be encouraged to ask for help privately after class. There is a protocol for this: they should set a specific time when they will be the focus of the teacher's attention, rather than accosting a teacher in the hallway. We know that the longer a student delays asking for help, the more pronounced the problem is likely to become. The gap between last week's lesson and today's grows larger. In subjects such as math, where information is cumulative, and each lesson builds upon the previous one, it doesn't take long to feel way behind. Many students talk about knowing the information or the facts but stumbling when it comes to applying that information on a test that asks them to go beyond what they have learned and problem-solve beyond the facts. Students need, first of all, to understand what is going wrong in their approach and learn the strategy it takes to push the envelope of learning in a particular discipline. Time spent solo with a teacher can help them see where their learning is breaking down and enable them to understand what is expected.

Parents can also be helpful in suggesting sources for academic support and help. We all know that some teachers are by nature more accessible and helpful than others. Some are caregivers as well as purveyors of information. So we advise students experiencing academic difficulty to begin by asking the teacher for help. As with making an appointment, however, there is a protocol for this.

Students too often make the mistake of beginning such a session by complaining about their grade. This is off-putting to the teacher. The insinuation is that a higher grade is deserved, which can be heard as a criticism or a challenge to the teacher's judgment.

It is more effective if the student begins by saying that he or she wants to do better in the course. Maybe the grades do not seem to be reflecting how much the student enjoys the course or how well he or she does in other courses.

The student and teacher may reach an agreement that the student simply does not have the background or innate skills to keep up with the expectations of the teacher or the material. Teachers would love it if their students developed a love for the subject similar to their own. They often go into teaching to share the joy that they experience from their discipline. Many students—and parents—react to a low grade by blaming the teacher, which may or may not be valid. Nevertheless, it does not fix the problem. Like students, teachers have their own styles. There are cases where parents need to intervene in discussions about grades and learning styles, especially where there is a clash between wills. But parents should let the student have as much communication with the teacher as the situation allows before taking over. Sometimes constructive discussion with the student present, while not always easy, leads to a better understanding on the part of teacher and student as to how to reconcile styles, needs, and expectations.

There are times when, for a variety of reasons, a student and family need to go outside the school for extra help. A teacher may not respond to a student's pleas for help or may not have sufficient time to give after school.

Other resources include teachers from neighboring schools or colleges who are willing to tutor privately; upperclassmen from the student's high school or college students from a local institution; professional tutors and coaches who work for organizations such as Inspirica, the Princeton Review, Advantage Testing, Stanley Kaplan, Sylvan Learning Centers, Ivy Prep, Ivy Bound, Huntington Learning Centers, and many others.

A professional tutor can be objective and respect the line between doing the work for the student and guiding the student to do his/her best work. Professional tutors and homework helpers are best chosen, in our opinion, by reputation. Rely on word of mouth from satisfied customers in your area. Consult guidance counselors or educational counselors for recommendations, as over the years they see many professionals who have stood the test of time. They may also have a sense of what personality or instructional style might be most effective in working with your child. Let's face it. We have all had the experience of learning better from some instructors than from others. All other factors being equal, it can boil down to the chemistry between two people.

Many schools also have learning specialists on staff who can help with study skills, time management, exam study, and writing. These specialists are convenient and know from within what many teachers in the high school expect.

Every student must learn how to designate adequate time for study. Many students talk about working through the night when what they really mean is that they have spent a long, long time on homework, allowing frequent interruptions. It feels as though they have worked for six hours when in reality only two of those have been maximally productive. Learning is work. It calls for concentration and focus. Each student needs to find the rhythm of study that works for her. Not every student can sustain long periods of study without a break of fifteen or twenty minutes. Students need help realizing the difference between merely putting in time and studying effectively.

ʼ EXAM STUDY

Study for exams calls for a particular kind of preparation. Exams tend to require synthesis and integration of material learned, not rote feedback. A mentor of mine freshman year of college was actually the first instructor to teach me a successful approach to exam study. He advised that as I read the material for English day by day, I form my own index cards on which I would, in my own words, boil down what I had read, rephrasing the material and making connections between one class discussion and another as they occurred to me. This was a way of making my own what I was reading and learning in class. These cards became invaluable study tools before a comprehensive term exam. He also taught me to anticipate the kinds of essay topics likely to be derived from the material being studied, based on the major themes and emphases of the course. I would try to formulate my own essay topics and outline answers to them. Even if what was asked on the exam was not identical to what I had prepared, I had studied with an eye for meaningful themes and found details to back up my claims. This is interactive learning between the student and the material, as opposed to sponge-like absorption without original thoughts. Too often students are not learning the material when studying for an exam but merely poring over it without trying to make sense of it in the larger framework of the course. A successful student learns to make connections between topics or ideas, to look for patterns, to anticipate subsequent and related questions arising from discussion, and to go beyond what has been presented to engage in original thinking.

· BOARDING SCHOOL STUDENTS

Students in boarding schools have a natural advantage when it comes to seeking extra help. Study hours are set times for everyone on campus with teachers in attendance and available for help. This is one reason among many that families consider boarding school an option—learning and support are more integrated into the residential experience, more or less eliminating the need for outside tutors. This is, however, a big decision that affects the family dynamic. If a family does decide to explore this alternative to day school, the ideal time to make the switch is when the student is going into grade nine or ten, allowing time before the pivotal eleventh grade for the student to adapt to the change and the unfamiliar academic and social expectations.

· SUMMER SCHOOL AND THE POSTGRADUATE YEAR

It is sometimes necessary or advisable to repair a low grade, especially one below a C, by attending summer school. Both day and boarding schools offer this choice. Some students choose to take a summer course to advance in a sequence. For instance, the student who has been in a lower math track and will therefore be unable to take calculus in senior year may wish to study precalculus in a summer program in order to advance to calculus in the fall. A family needs to be sure that their high school approves this plan and is willing to recognize the proposed course as a prerequisite. Other students choose to repeat a course to show themselves, and potential colleges, that they can do it, thereby restoring their self-confidence in a less pressured circumstance, outside the normal high school curriculum where many courses are taken concurrently.

It is more difficult to repair an entire disappointing school year than to raise a single disappointing grade in one course. If the lower grades are in the ninth grade, the first year of meeting the demands of high school, that is perhaps of less concern than if low grades haunt the tenth- and eleventh-grade records. A poor record in tenth or eleventh grades may argue for a postgraduate, or thirteenth year, usually in a new school. Families should discuss this with school personnel, advisors, teachers, or an educational consultant to understand what is behind the low achievement before leaping into a postgraduate year. Many boarding schools offer this opportunity. It is important to consider the advisability of this option for the individual student, based on his or her maturity, commitment to this plan, and willingness to subject him/herself to the rules and regulations of boarding school and dorm living for one year. Otherwise, a year and $30,000 later, not much will have changed in terms of prospects for college. Many students have all they can do to endure four years of high school, let alone five! Unless the student is willing to buy into a possible dress code, lights out, weekend restrictions, and strict policies on substance use, an extra year of high school will just be an expensive indulgence.

· THE STUDENT WITH INCONSISTENT GRADES

As the work becomes increasingly difficult, more conceptual and abstract, from eighth grade through senior year, many students struggle to maintain the high level of academic achievement they had attained previously. Their record in grades nine or ten may not be as impressive as it was in middle school. By following the advice in the previous pages about increasing awareness of how one learns and learning to accept appropriate help, students can stay on top of their game. As self-awareness increases, so do grades.

Some colleges, such as Princeton, do not factor results from ninth grade into their admission decisions. Most, however, do, viewing the first three years of high school as an arc of learning, look for an upward trend. Thus there is hope for the student who blooms later, finding his or her academic stride in the course of high school—preferably before senior year!—but better late than never.

The eleventh grade is a pivotal year, the last full year before colleges make their decision to admit or deny. Colleges expect that by then a student will have discovered seriousness of purpose, sustaining a solid level of performance. It is very important that courses for the eleventh grade be thoughtfully chosen to make sure that the right combination for success is struck. This has been fully discussed in the first chapter.

Prospective employers have increasingly asked job applicants to include the high school GPA on their résumé. Students who do not view college as the next step after high school should therefore not assume that academic success is unimportant.

ALTERNATIVES TO TRADITIONAL HIGH SCHOOL:
ABOVE AND BEYOND

When we hear the phrases *special needs* or *extra help*, we assume that they refer to students who have learning issues that require extra support or accommodations. Many high school students need a different kind of help. They are not enjoying learning because they are under-challenged and, therefore, unmotivated. Some are more experiential, hands-on learners who are easily bored by unmitigated textbook learning that they view as irrelevant to them or to which they cannot connect. Their *special needs* are for a more demanding or creative curriculum and school experience, one with a different orientation than most traditional classrooms. What can parents do to help this type of student find maximum academic satisfaction, especially when alternatives cannot be supplied within the school?

Begin by speaking with teachers and administrators who know your child. See if there is a way to supplement the curriculum with creative or individual research projects that a teacher would be willing to supervise. Colleges respect the initiative and commitment demonstrated by a student's taking on an independent study project. That same teacher might well become a source of a strong personal recommendation for college applications, because a one-on-one relationship allows him or her to know the student's thinking, work ethic, imagination, and capacity for research and independent work, all of which are so important in college.

Explore alternatives outside the school. Is there a community college nearby that offers courses in an area of interest? Even if this does not become a formal part of the student's high school transcript, when it comes time to apply to colleges, a separate transcript of this college course can be included.

If alternatives such as these cannot be put in place, a change of school may be advisable. This is a big decision. It should be conducted with careful and thoughtful attention to the pros and cons of this move. Any change is bound to generate some uncertainty and anxiety. A student needs to understand the reasons for such a move and agree that its merits outweigh its drawbacks, such as leaving friends.

· ALTERNATIVES TO TRADITIONAL HIGH SCHOOL

Early College High Schools exist in twenty-five states, sponsored by the Bill and Melinda Gates Foundation, the Carnegie Corporation of New York, and the W. K.

Kellogg Foundation. These schools provide challenging courses with appropriate support.

Bard High School Early College represents a relatively recent option. In this program students can earn both a high school degree and a two-year associate of arts degree during the four years of high school. This alternative is clearly only for highly motivated students. But parents looking to diversify the experience of high school should search for models of this type that may exist locally.

High Mountain Institute in Colorado and the Mountain School in Vermont provide an alternative for students who wish to take a break from their home school and spend a semester or a year in an academically demanding yet environmentally different setting.

A school such as Simon's Rock Early College—associated with Bard College (located in Great Barrington, Massachusetts)—is an alternative to high school for successful students who have completed tenth grade. It honors intellectual and social development on an individual basis by offering liberal arts and some recently introduced technical, business, and professional programs to students younger than most typical freshmen.

Early Entrance is an option at many colleges. This alternative is suitable for students who have successfully completed junior year and have fulfilled all graduation requirements except for senior English. Upon completing freshman English in college, usually with a grade of B or higher, the high school diploma can be received retroactively. To qualify for Early Entrance, a student would need to have taken the SAT I or ACT if the college requires standardized testing. Students who are merely trying to flee the restrictions imposed by life at home or the requirements of high school and students who are socially ill adjusted will not likely fare well in the Early Entrance process. Colleges are looking for well-adjusted, primarily academically successful students who have exhausted the resources of high school and are ready for more.

Early Colleges (http://www.earlycolleges.org) is a program that sets up small schools that permit a student to complete high school while earning two years of college credit. It specifically targets low-income students, ESL learners, students of color, and first-generation students.

College and High School Partnerships exist where colleges offer courses taught by approved high school teachers at their own school. These are available in nearly every state now, through colleges such as Indiana University, Kenyon College, the University of Minnesota, the University of Pittsburg, and Syracuse University. Some, but not all, colleges accept college credits for these courses; regardless, such courses are an effective way to add stimulation to a high school curriculum.

The International Baccalaureate (http:// www.ibo.org) provides a classic education akin to that of the last two years of many European secondary schools. A student may sample IB courses in areas of special interest, receiving a certificate for this work, or work toward the IB diploma with six courses a year in literature, foreign language, social science, experimental science, math, and the arts. The IB is offered at over 500 high schools in the United States, about 90 percent of them public. If available, this option for highly motivated students is a rare opportunity to deepen learning and give the student an edge in the college application process. There is a cost to the family of $620 per student.

Some students choose to complete high school without earning a traditional diploma. Instead, they sit for the General Education Development (GED) test, available almost anywhere in the United States and Canada, as well as at over one hundred international sites. The GED measures a student's academic skills in a high school curriculum against those of traditional high school students. Prep books and prep courses do exist to address the requirements of this exam.

There are also online diploma alternatives such as Capitol High School or Thomson High School Diploma, accredited by the Middle States Commission on Secondary Schools. The Thomson Diploma includes career-oriented electives, such as auto repair technician and personal computer specialist, in addition to traditional academic studies, such as English, math, world history, and science, among others.

If a student has certain colleges in mind, it is advisable to check their specific admission policies regarding high school equivalency degrees.

' HOME SCHOOLING

A somewhat extreme, but increasingly popular, alternative to traditional high school is homeschooling. Following in the footsteps of such notables as Benjamin Franklin, Abigail Adams, and Patrick Henry, students who are homeschooled can determine with their instructors the style and pace of the curriculum, to a certain extent. The number of families choosing to home school their children is growing rapidly. Some families home school because of religious conviction, some because they are seeking more rigorous academic standards than they have found in their community schools, some because they want to change their child's social environment, and some because they want to address the specific needs of their child, especially if they live in an area with few alternatives.

There are many Web sites on the topic of homeschooling that describe where to locate curricula and materials, review guides such as Mary Pride's *Complete Guide to Homeschooling*, or the Pearson Learning Group Books and Programs. Some homeschooling curricula are sponsored and overseen by major universities, such as the University of Nebraska–Lincoln. Within this structure, university staff professors evaluate exams.

Most colleges have proven receptive to homeschooled applicants whose studies have included traditional academic courses easily recognizable to admission committees. Homeschooled students do have a responsibility to develop interests and join activities outside of their studies. A large component of college life is social and involves getting along with people of different backgrounds and cultures, not studying and existing in an insular environment, so it is important to develop interactive involvements. This capability is also *very* important to prospective employers.

INTERNATIONAL STUDENTS STUDYING IN THE UNITED STATES: CROSSOVER

High school students from other countries or American high school students living abroad who plan to apply to colleges and universities in the United States need to accomplish a few tasks in order to be serious applicants.

If English is not a first language, foreign students will need to register for the Test of English as a Foreign Language (TOEFL) and take it before December of the year they are processing applications. Since the TOEFL can be taken more than once, it makes good sense to take it early so that if a second administration is advisable, there is time to schedule it.

The TOEFL is a three-and-a-half-hour-long examination that can be computer-based or paper-based. To locate centers, students can call 1-800-468-6335 for the United States, United States territories, and Canada, or they can contact the Regional Registration Center for the country in which they live. Students who plan to take the exam in the United States but wish to arrange for that from another country should call 1-443-751-4862. Free test-preparation materials can be downloaded from the TOEFL Web site at www.ets.org/toefl. Walk-in scheduling is also available. Consult the TOEFL Information and Registration Bulletin for further details. Since September 2005 the new TOEFL test has included speaking tasks as well as listening, reading, and writing. Applicants should refer to www.ets.org/ell for further online resources to enhance English language skills.

The TOEFL consists of three sections: listening comprehension, structure and written expression, and reading comprehension. Each section has a time limit. On the paper-based test there is a thirty-minute writing test, in which the student writes a short essay on a topic provided.

Some transcripts will require an official translation into English. This must be done using a certified service, which can be located on the internet under Transcript Translation. There are two types of services—those that do translations and those that do evaluations. An evaluation lists equivalents to U.S. grades and courses. Students should check with each college in which they are interested to see what is required. The Web site lists Josef Silny & Associates (www.jsilny.com) as one service that does both a translation and an evaluation.

Foreign students reading the section of this book titled *Developing Interests and Activities* may feel that their schools do not offer the same opportunities as U.S. high schools to be involved in clubs, organizations, and community service. If your high school does not offer these kinds of opportunities, it becomes your responsibility to develop a commitment to sports, community service, or some organization or club outside of school. U.S. colleges are aware of these cultural differences, but that does not mean that an empty résumé will be altogether excused.

While preparation for the standardized tests required by U.S. colleges is very accessible in the United States, it may not be so readily obtainable in some foreign countries. It is important in the tenth grade to begin thinking about how you will help your child structure test prep. The section in this book titled *Standardized Exams: Put to the Test* addresses the different types of preparation, from self-study to formal tutoring. The key is to begin early enough to allow for a testing schedule that is spread out over the eleventh and twelfth grades, so that cramming is avoided.

International students will also have to apply for a passport if they do not already have one and obtain a visa application form from the U.S. embassy or consulate three months before arriving to enroll in a U.S. college.

The College Board's International Education office in Washington DC provides support and detailed information on the process of applying to a U.S. college. Its e-mail is: Internatl@collegeboard.org.

LEARNING STYLES:
PEELING THE LABEL

Each of us learns differently. Many children, however, have difficulty of a certain kind, be it processing speed, decoding, manipulating mathematical symbols, spelling, or auditory processing that makes keeping up with grade-level expectations challenging, at best, or impossible, at worst. Some children exhibit complex combinations of learning difficulties. Those who do not learn fairly easily in a traditional way, whose learning makes keeping up with their peers a Sisyphean task, often mask their frustration, humiliation, or feelings of inadequacy by pretending that academics don't much matter to them. In common parlance, they *tune out*. Their attitude toward school may range from one of indifference to one of disdain for, and resistance to, authority. It is important for parents to determine early on if their child has a learning difference that will qualify for test accommodations.

Deep down, everyone wants to do well, to succeed at something. Parents of children with learning differences will face particular challenges—partly because our educational systems are not very flexible on the whole—as they try to help their son or daughter develop understanding and confidence as a learner.

A psychologist or learning specialist can administer a battery of tests—termed a psycho-educational evaluation—made up of a standard age-appropriate IQ test and various subtests to measure reading speed, dexterity, reading comprehension, mathematical computation, and visual-spatial aptitude, among many other learning components. If deemed advisable, psychological tests can be administered to evaluate deficient social judgment, phobias, resistant or hostile behavior, or immaturity. Oftentimes there is an emotional side to learning problems that may either cause academic frustration or failure or be a consequence of them.

Such an evaluation is critical to diagnose a child with ADD (Attention Deficit Disorder) or ADHD (with Hyperactivity). Much has been written about the various qualities and characteristics that define a learning difference or that justify the labels of ADD or ADHD. I will not attempt to cover that ground here. Instead, I refer you to four excellent, readable books by experts in learning differences:

Hallowell, Edward M. and Ratey, John J. *Delivered from Distraction*.New York, New York: Ballantine Books, 2005.

Koplewicz, Harold. *It's Nobody's Fault*. New York, New York: Three Rivers Press, 1997.

Levine, Mel. *All Kinds of Minds*. New York, New York: Simon & Shuster, 2002.

Shaywitz, Sally. *Overcoming Dyslexia.* New York, New York: Alfred A. Knopf, 2003.

One question that troubles parents of children with learning differences is whether or not disclosing that learning style will label the student unhelpfully throughout high school and into college.

If standardized tests, such as the SAT I, SAT IIs, or the ACT will need to be administered with accommodations in order for a student to show his/her best results, then the student must be on file with the high school as both qualifying for, and using, accommodations of some sort. The College Board (ETS) and ACT require a letter from the student's high school verifying that a need for accommodations has been authentically and professionally ascertained. So, if it will help a student to receive accommodations in high school, and they qualify for them, it makes sense to give those students that advantage.

There is no designation on the score report indicating that the test has been taken under special circumstances. By law there cannot be. Therefore, the decision of whether or not to disclose a learning style difference to colleges has more to do with a student's need for support and accommodation once enrolled than it does with the application process itself. Why should a student find him/herself at a college without adequate academic resource support or at a school with instructors insensitive to the issue of learning differences and therefore reluctant or even unwilling to give them extended time for tests?

More important than any of the considerations pertaining to the student as college applicant are those that have to do with the student as a learner. Identifying a nontraditional learning style may well be the first step toward helping the student to succeed academically. There are many interventions that can show a student how she/ he learns best. Medication may be the right solution for some students, but finding the correct medication and the right dosage can be frustrating and time-consuming. For others, study and reading techniques teach them how to claim ownership of the material and how to develop effective study habits and organizational skills. Students who feel comfortable admitting the need for help can be taught to ask for it without feeling inferior. They are at much lower risk for academic difficulty in the independent atmosphere of college than the student left to cover up the need for support and intervention.

When it comes time to consider college, it is better to have earned higher grades and to receive higher scores on standardized tests than to have received more modest grades and to struggle, out of pride, to take exams without necessary accommodations and achieve lower scores.

Over 50 percent of U.S. college students use support services during the course of their four-year college career. Colleges vary significantly in the amount of support they provide, but even highly selective colleges offer support of some kind, varying from peer tutoring by upperclassmen to full-fledged professional help from learning specialists. References that will help you determine where support is offered are:

Mangrum, Charles T. and Strichart, Stephen S. (eds.). *Peterson's Colleges with Programs for Students with Learning Disabilities or Attention Deficit Disorders.* Princeton, NJ: Peterson's, 2003.

Kravets, Marybeth and Wax, Imy F. *The K & W Guide to Colleges for Students with Learning Disabilities or Attention Deficit Disorder.* New York, New York: Random House, Inc., 1997.

Families need to research thoroughly the support service offered by a high school or college. The best research of all is an actual visit to the resource room to discuss with resident personnel your child's specific needs. Does the student feel a comfortable connection to the people staffing the resource room? Does the actual space feel airy and light or depressing? Is the service compatible with your daughter or son's needs?

Those students who have obtained high grades and high test scores despite a learning difference (colleges publish the median scores of admitted students in the various college indexes) should, in general, experience no notable difference in the college application process compared with students without learning differences. When a student's standardized scores are significantly lower than published medians, he or she might begin to look at the many colleges that do not require standardized tests.

Students who have worked hard over the high school years to come to grips with how they learn often turn into conscientious, disciplined, dedicated students who do very well. They know how and when to ask for help and realize that learning is not necessarily easy. They are willing to work hard for their grades. They do not take homework for granted. Colleges with experience admitting students with learning differences know that the odds are very good that they value academic achievement and will use resources intelligently once on campus.

Anyone who reads Mel Levine's *All Kinds of Minds* will learn that children who learn differently often bring to the classroom and to their approach to assignments a different way of seeing or understanding an issue that can be highly enlightening to others. They are often highly imaginative, creative learners whose presence is a real asset.

The topic of learning differences is highly complex and sensitive. Our point in raising it here is to assure parents that there is a wide range of reception to different learning styles among high schools and colleges. If disclosing this difference increases the student's confidence as a learner and his or her chances for academic success, making learning more possible or perhaps even fun, then that is the recommended pathway to follow. It does not hurt chances for success in the college application process, providing the right colleges are chosen.

TABLE TALK:
PARENTS WALK THE LINE

Parents have a difficult job assessing their role as guides to their children as they travel through high school. They must learn to walk the line between being seen as intrusive and being seen as helpful.

We parents are inevitably going to make some mistakes along the way. Adolescents appear very needy one day and disdainful of our attention or affection the next. It is sometimes challenging to make the right judgment call. Adolescents are best understood as looking forward toward the unfamiliar and the unknown while at the same time casting glances over their shoulder toward the comfort of the recent past. The best advice for parents is to sharpen your listening skills and trust your instincts. It is often much more important to listen than to know exactly what to say. You know your children better than anybody else. Don't let anyone tell you otherwise. When something doesn't seem right in their behavior or attitude, go for it!

We do, however, need at times to temper our expectations for their success. Success needs to be defined individually for each child, not by our exacting or inflexible standards. We cannot judge success by general standards such as an SAT I score, National Honor Society selection, or a winning goal. There are many, many ways to be successful.

We also have to check the impulse to over identify with our children's successes and failures. Of course, victory is sweet and failure stings, but a missed social opportunity or missed tennis serve is not life-threatening. Keep it in perspective, and in doing so, help your child to keep a healthy perspective, too. Help them to see what happens in a larger, overall context of a life being lived, of a personality emerging. Any one decision or event along the way is just that—only one event. Some are more consequential than others, to be sure, but success cannot be easily defined by one triumph or one victory; it is made up of many actions and decisions over time. An arc of experience begins to form, defining our children as students, and as people, instilling both knowledge and values.

Seeking what we view as best for our children, we parents often fixate on one test or one class election as the decisive moment that will determine our child's future. Children are on the whole very resilient. While we still burn for their loss, still hold anger toward the teacher who on Tuesday failed to see our boy's genius, by Thursday our son most probably has moved on and forgotten the episode, while we continue to feel protective.

The temptation to make excuses for our child's missed deadline or forgotten essay is strong. We would like the consequences of those slip-ups not to be long-lasting, for the class grade not to be so strongly affected by this oversight that it slips a whole level. We do our children no favor by covering up for them or being accountable for them instead of teaching them to be accountable. In fact, the unspoken message when we do is that it is okay to make up excuses for lapses in responsibility. In the long run, a student makes a more positive impression on authority figures by facing up to the negligence and accepting the consequences, learning from the experience. This is difficult when we look around and see other parents making up excuses to get their child off the hook, but by speaking for our children instead of teaching them how to speak for themselves, we actually deprive them of the chance to develop their own strong voice and their own negotiating skills.

In the college application process, students whose parents take control and are ventriloquists for them do not usually fare well in the process because they are applicants with little investment in the process. They never declare who they are. When you hear the mythic story of the seemingly perfect applicant who did not get into a top-choice college, ask yourself if her parents might have subsumed her role.

Some parents like to collude with the teacher, counselor, or principal instead of involving the student in the issue under discussion. I call them *whisperers*. They like to script the agenda of a meeting or session beforehand, manipulating the outcome, rather than allowing open discussion and exchange to see what comes out of the meeting. They preclude the possibility of original outcomes. This practice is insulting to the professionals involved and to your child of high school age. Put the concerns on the table with all parties involved a part of the process. When parents take over, students become indifferent, disconnected, sometimes resentful or resistant to change. Our role is to help our sons and daughters make thoughtful, reasonable, safe decisions, not always to make them for them.

Parents need to remember that *things have changed* since they went to college. We cannot let nostalgia for our college days color the process for our children. The Dartmouth, Smith, or Hamilton of today is not exactly the school we may have known. In the film *What's Eating Gilbert Grape*, the mother, debilitated by being very overweight, says upon meeting her son's girlfriend for the first time, "I didn't always look this way." It is a wonderfully resonant line that points out that our children don't necessarily think or look beyond the way they perceive us in the present to the time when we were their age, going through problems as they are now. Similarly, parents tend to view their children as young, not as the adults they are becoming. Finding a realistic point of view, fair to both sides, is a constant challenge during the high school years. Parents and children need to work together to understand where the other's opinions are coming from.

Success takes work by each party—parents and children. It doesn't just happen. We have to help our children define what they themselves believe makes them feel successful. It will mean different things to different students and families. To some, success may be popularity or athletic prowess. To others, it may be looking buff or svelte. Getting all A's may be another student's primary goal. When parents see their son or daughter looking unhappy, it can be difficult to learn what is causing the distress. The girl whose best friend has turned catty, the boy not selected for varsity tennis, the student chosen for the chorus but not to star in the school musical—any loss like these can lead to poor academic performance. Most adolescents are reluctant to talk to parents about social and academic misfires. The parent sees the sadness, sullenness, or anger but cannot get at its cause. The student who has someone to talk to other than the parents, such as a close friend, older sib, therapist, trusted teacher or counselor, coach, or minister has an advantage when disappointment, sadness, or hurt enters his or her life. The teen already isolated among peers can suffer deeply over feelings of rejection, humiliation, failure, or exclusion. Parents need to be careful not to convey their own disappointment by over identifying with their child's performance, thereby intensifying the feelings of failure.

A chemistry test given in the midst of such emotional turmoil seems to have little relevance. Long-range perspective is difficult to establish in the young, who tend to live in the immediate moment. We struggle to help them see beyond their disappointment or hurt to the day when having done well on that chemistry test will again seem important. This is the time for parents to reach out to someone in the child's life who can take notice of their mood and discuss it with them. It is okay in these circumstances to ask a trusted teacher or friend to intercede and show that someone has noticed the change and cares enough about it to ask if they can help, if only by listening. Parents should not take it personally that, at this stage of development, when their son or daughter sees asking Mom or Dad for help as regressive to their growing independence, they may not be able to take as direct a role as they would like. What is important more than who helps is that someone is there to help, to provide a channel for communication.

In some cases, wounded by social slings, worried about family, confused by the disconnection between effort and results, a student may at some level of consciousness decide to fail. This decision may be a cry for attention or a desperate act to bring parents together over a crisis. It may be paralysis in the face of frustration. It is certainly a time for parents to seek understanding and intervention from a professional who knows their child, be it a pediatrician or therapist, or else a relative or family friend. When grades begin to plummet or a child's social behavior shifts, quick action is called for, before lost academic ground is harder to recover or irreversible social behavior develops. Lack of academic or social success is not always about ability or capacity; often it will have an emotional cause.

IN SUMMARY

While arranging weekly dinners with your children may be a scheduling challenge, this ritual provides a critical time for communication and connection. This is especially true during times of stress over a school issue. Parents should not ever use this time to address school issues. You may think that asking, "How'd the math test go today?" is a perfectly innocent question, expressing your concern and interest. Heard, however, as, "How'd you do on today's math test?" or, worse yet, "What grade do you think you got?" it can be explosive. Dinner is virtually over at that point, to the sound of a door slamming hard! Only the student is permitted to bring school topics to the table. If she does, that is a clear sign that she needs to talk about them. Parents need to be ready to listen and save advice for a later time, after reflection. In lieu of dinnertime together, shopping, a car ride, or sports event can provide a substitute, though there does seem to be something nurturing about food! But the same rule applies: use this time for family stories, memories, gossip about weird Uncle Ned, observations about the world—anything but school.

For some reason, the subject of high school seems replete with words that begin with the letter *p*. Just think about it: pressure, principal, programs, participation, PSAT, prep, performance, pass, potential, parents, and physics. I am sure you can think of more. If high school is resourcefully and thoughtfully experienced, no spin doctor has to be called in to *package* young people. Instead, self-direction, purposeful decision-making, academic achievement, meaningful involvement in activities, will lead to effective self-presentation in essays, interviews, and in the overall application.

WHAT MATTERS MOST TO COLLEGES: THE NEXT STEP

It is difficult in a book about success in high school not to talk about the next step for a majority of graduates—college. Our primary focus is maximizing the experience of high school—to show parents how to help their children feel empowered by making choices and decisions that will serve them well both in high school and beyond. We want them to learn how to learn, to enjoy learning, and to develop leadership skills and activities that will serve them their life long. And to have a good time doing all this.

If a senior decides to apply for some form of higher education after high school, it is impossible to reverse what three years of high school have set up as a profile or transcript of that applicant. The boy slow to mature and take studies seriously or the girl naive about the expectation for demonstrated leadership or community service cannot put those accomplishments in place at the last minute. I frequently meet a junior whose ninth-

and tenth-grade records are lackluster for want of trying but who wants to believe that a strong eleventh grade will erase that history and make Yale stand up and take notice. This is magical thinking. While an upward trend in grades and accomplishments is decidedly beneficial to the college applicant, highly selective colleges are seeing such a glut of qualified applicants in their pools that they cannot be so forgiving of two years of weak grades.

The student with this profile might do well to consider attending the best college that admits him, where he can do well and achieve an impressive record in one, one and a half, or two years that would argue for transferring up the ladder in selectivity. This two-step approach can eventually land many students at the college of their dreams. But college grades must be above a 3.5, in most cases, to enter selective colleges.

When a college evaluates a student's accomplishments in high school, what factors are considered most important? Most colleges would rank them, more or less, as follows:

- Grades in all academic courses, from ninth grade through the first quarter or first half of senior year. (A few colleges, such as Princeton, do not consider ninth grade.)

- Grades in Honors, Advanced, AP, or IB courses

- Class rank, if provided by the school

- Strength of curriculum

- Standardized test scores (not relevant for some colleges)

- Teacher and college counselor recommendations

- Student essays
- Demonstrated leadership, community service, meaningful activities
- Interviews (where given)
- Variables such as gender, geography, minority status, exceptional sports or musical talent, legacy status, a family history of generous donations

It is nearly impossible to generalize about the importance of the variables listed above in the admission process. They vary considerably by school. Legacy status is highly regarded at almost every college and can increase considerably a qualified student's chances of being admitted. Some experts believe that legacy status at many schools can almost double a student's odds of being accepted, especially if she applies Early Decision.

There is no one formula to follow that guarantees acceptance to the college of choice. Following the advice in the previous pages, however, will increase the likelihood.

Colleges like to see that students have developed an appreciation of, if not a love for, learning; taken advantage of opportunities to explore interests and develop talents; exposed themselves to different cultures and customs; and developed socially as well as academically.

We as parents and educators can be thankful if the high school years have been a time of healthy intellectual and personal growth for our children. Every child will develop differently. Some will be ready sooner than others to get more out of high school. But most children can get more out of high school if helped to understand how.

They need to understand why it is important, given the next step of college or the work force, to graduate having realized their capabilities, having developed oral and written expression, and having learned to think critically and creatively.

Not everyone will leave high school and attend Yale, Stanford, or Harvard. Not everyone will choose to attend college at all. Not everyone should, at least not directly out of high school. But every student deserves to leave high school saying it was an important time of life and a significant stage in their development. What we as parents want for our sons and daughters is that they make good and right choices to help them make the most of high school.

APPENDIX
A LIST OF RECOMMENDED
BOOKS FOR HIGH SCHOOL
READERS

Amidst predictions of the death of the novel and of reading for pleasure's sake becoming an extinct activity within the next few decades, people, nevertheless, continue to read, for pleasure as well as for information. To be reminded of the importance of reading, one has only to recall the desperate outreach for books by the characters in Ray Bradbury's *Fahrenheit 451* when they are forbidden and burned. The list compiled below represents a broad spectrum of authors, cultural backgrounds, styles, and time periods, ranging from Homer, Shakespeare, and Defoe to Billy Collins, Edward Albee, and Michael Crichton. It attempts to appeal to a variety of literary tastes and interests. We hope that it serves as a starting point from which to pick and choose fiction and nonfiction, drama and poetry. These works have either stood the test of time or have a good chance of doing so—largely because they touch on universal truths about the human heart and spirit or because they entertain, or both. Whether one reads *Beowulf* or *Lord of the Flies*, Plato or Stephen Hawking, most important is the act of reading itself: the mind and imagination engaged in the solitary, reflective process of interacting with another intelligence rendered through language.

FICTION

Chinua Achebe, *Things Fall Apart*

James Agee, *A Death in the Family*

Isabel Allende, *Portrait in Sepia*

Jane Austen, *Pride and Prejudice*

James Baldwin, *Go Tell It on the Mountain*

L. Frank Baum, *The Wizard of Oz*

Saul Bellow, *The Adventures of Augie March; Seize the Day*

Ray Bradbury, *Dandelion Wine; Something Wicked this Way Comes*

Charlotte Brontë, *Jane Eyre*

Emily Brontë, *Wuthering Heights*

Dan Brown, *The Da Vinci Code*

Anthony Burgess, *A Clockwork Orange*

Albert Camus, *The Stranger*

Caleb Carr, *The Alienist*

Willa Cather, *Death Comes for the Archbishop; O Pioneers!*

Kate Chopin, *The Awakening*

Sandra Cisneros, *The House on Mango Street*

James Clavell, *Shogun*

Joseph Conrad, *Heart of Darkness; Lord Jim*

James Fenimore Cooper, *The Last of the Mohicans*

Michael Crichton, *The Andromeda Strain; Congo; Jurassic Park*

Robert Cormier, *The Chocolate War*

Stephen Crane, *The Red Badge of Courage*

Daniel Defoe, *Robinson Crusoe*

Charles Dickens, *A Tale of Two Cities; David Copperfield; Great Expectations*

E. L. Doctorow, *Ragtime*

Fyodor Dostoyevsky, *Crime and Punishment*

Arthur Conan Doyle, *The Adventures of Sherlock Holmes*

Andre Dubus III, *House of Sand and Fog*

Daphne du Maurier, *Rebecca*

George Eliot, *Middlemarch; The Mill on The Floss; Silas Marner*

Ralph Ellison, *Invisible Man*

Louise Erdrich, *The Antelope Wife; The Beet Queen; The Bingo Palace*

William Faulkner, *Light in August*

F. Scott Fitzgerald, *The Great Gatsby*

E. M. Forster, *A Passage to India*

Charles Frazier, *Cold Mountain*

Gustave Flaubert, *Madame Bovary*

William Golding, *Lord of the Flies*

John Grisham, *The Firm*

Alex Haley, *Roots*

Thomas Hardy, *The Mayor of Casterbridge*

Nathaniel Hawthorne, *The Scarlet Letter*

Joseph Heller, *Catch-22*

Ernest Hemingway, *A Farewell to Arms, The Old Man and the Sea*

Frank Herbert, *Dune*

Herman Hesse, *Siddhartha*

Khaled Hosseini, *The Kite Runner*

Victor Hugo, *The Hunchback of Notre Dame*

Zora Neale Hurston, *Their Eyes Were Watching God*

Aldous Huxley, *Brave New World*

John Irving, *A Prayer For Owen Meany; The World According to Garp*

Henry James, *Daisy Miller; The Turn of the Screw*

James Joyce, *Portrait of the Artist as a Young Man; The Dubliners*

Franz Kafka, *Metamorphosis; The Trial*

Ken Kesey, *One Flew over the Cuckoo's Nest*

Stephen King, *Misery*

John Knowles, *A Separate Peace*

Jhumpa Lahiri, *Interpreter of Maladies*

Harper Lee, *To Kill a Mockingbird*

Jack London, *The Call of the Wild*

Norman Maclean, *A River Runs Through It*

Norman Mailer, *The Naked and the Dead*

Bernard Malamud, *The Natural*

Thomas Mann, *The Magic Mountain*

Gabriel Garcia Márquez, *One Hundred Years of Solitude*

Catherine Marshall, *Christy*

Herman Melville, *Billy Budd; Moby-Dick*

Toni Morrison, *Beloved; The Bluest Eye*

V. S. Naipaul, *A Bend in the River*

Phyllis Reynolds Naylor, *Simply Alice*

Flannery O'Connor, *A Good Man Is Hard to Find*

George Orwell, *Animal Farm; 1984*

Walker Percy, *The Moviegoer*

Sylvia Plath, *The Bell Jar*

Edgar Allan Poe, *Selected Tales*

Erich Maria Remarque, *All Quiet on the Western Front*

J. D. Salinger, *The Catcher in the Rye; Nine Stories*

Dr. Seuss, *The Lorax*

Mary Shelley, *Frankenstein*

Leslie Marmon Silko, *Ceremony*

John Steinbeck, *The Grapes of Wrath*

Alexander Solzhenitsyn, *One Day in the Life of Ivan Denisovich*

Neville Shute, *On the Beach*

Jonathan Swift, *Gulliver's Travels*

J. R. Tolkien, *The Lord of the Rings*

Leo Tolstoy, *War and Peace*

Ivan Turgenev, *Fathers and Sons*

Mark Twain, *The Adventures of Huckleberry Finn*

John Updike, *Rabbit Run*

Kurt Vonnegut, Jr., *Cat's Cradle; Slaughter-House Five*

Alice Walker, *The Color Purple*

Robert Penn Warren, *All the King's Men*

Evelyn Waugh, *A Handful of Dust*

Eudora Welty, *Collected Stories*

Edith Wharton, *Ethan Frome; The House of Mirth*

T. H. White, *The Once and Future King*

Oscar Wilde, *The Portrait of Dorian Gray*

Thomas Wolfe, *The Right Stuff*

Virginia Woolf, *To the Lighthouse*

Richard Wright, *Native Son*

DRAMA

Edward Albee, *The Sandbox; Zoo Story; Who's Afraid of Virginia Woolf*

Samuel Beckett, *Waiting for Godot*

Anton Chekhov, *The Cherry Orchard*

Henrik Ibsen, *A Doll's House*

Eugene Ionesco, *Rhinoceros*

Frank C. Leana, PhD, and Carole S. Clark, MEd

Arthur Miller, *Death of a Salesman; The Crucible*

Eugene O'Neill, *Long Day's Journey into Night*

William Shakespeare, *Hamlet; Henry IV—Parts I & II; King Lear; Macbeth; A Midsummer Night's Dream; Romeo and Juliet; The Tempest*

George Bernard Shaw, *Heartbreak House; Pygmalion*

Sophocles, *Antigone; Oedipus Rex*

Tennessee Williams, *The Glass Menagerie: A Streetcar Named Desire*

POETRY

Beowulf, trans. by Seamus Heaney

Emily Dickinson, *Selected Poems*

Robert Frost, *Selected Poems*

Harold H. Henderson, *An Introduction to Haiku*

Homer, *The Iliad; The Odyssey,* trans. by Robert Fitzgerald

Virgil, *The Aeneid*

The Oxford books of American and English Poetry

NONFICTION

The Bible

Maya Angelou, *I Know Why the Caged Bird Sings*

Frank Conroy, *Stop-Time*

Lorene Carey, *Black Ice*

Robert Caro, *The Power Broker*

Jung Chang, *Wild Swans: Three Daughters of China*

Jared Diamond, *Guns, Germs, and Steel*

Charles Darwin, *Origin of Species*

Sarah and Elizabeth Delaney, *Having Our Say: The Delaney Sisters' First 100 Years*

Annie Dillard, *Pilgrim at Tinker Creek*

Loren Eisley, *The Immense Journey*

Ralph Waldo Emerson, *Selected Essays*

Benjamin Franklin, *The Autobiography of Benjamin Franklin*

Sigmund Freud, *The Interpretation of Dreams*

Doris Kearns Goodwin, *Wait Till Next Year: A Memoir*; *Team of Rivals: The Political Genius of Abraham Lincoln*

Stephen J. Gould, *The Mismeasure of Man*

Brian Greene, *The Elegant Universe*

David Halberstam, *The Best And the Brightest*

Stephen Hawking, *A Brief History of Time*

John F. Kennedy, *Profiles in Courage*

Alfred Lansing, *Endurance: Shackleton's Incredible Voyage*

Frank McCourt, *Angela's Ashes*

Malcolm X with Alex Haley, *Malcolm X*

Plato, *The Republic*

William Schirer , *The Rise and Fall of the Third Reich*

William Strunk & E. B. White, *The Elements of Style*

Ron Suskind, *A Hope in the Unseen*

Lewis Thomas, *Lives of A Cell*

Henry David Thoreau, *Walden*

James Thurber, *Carnival*

Barbara Tuchman, *The Guns of August*

Booker T. Washington, *Up from Slavery*

Elie Weisel, *Night*

Tobias Wolff, *This Boy's Life: A Memoir*

Sample Interview Questions

These questions help students to do an honest and thoughtful self-evaluation that will prepare them for statements they may be asked to make about themselves in a college admission interview. A successful interview is a dialogue that gives you an opportunity to show something of your personality and to share your ideas, points of view, and concerns. It is also important to show that you have done research about the college by consulting its Web site, reading its catalogue, or browsing through one of the guidebooks or indexes such as *The Fiske Guide to Colleges*, *The Yale Insider's Guide to Colleges*, or *Barron's Profiles of American Colleges*.

Goals and Values

What have you enjoyed the most about high school?

What have been your most important challenges or achievements? Of which are you proudest?

What do you value? What concerns take up most of your energy, time, effort, or thought?

How do you define success? What would you like to accomplish in the future?

What kind of person would you like to become? Of your gifts and strengths, which would you most like to develop? What would you change about yourself?

If you had a year to go anywhere and do anything, what would you choose to do?

What particular events or experiences have shaped your growth and ways of thinking?

EDUCATION

What are your academic interests? Which courses have you most enjoyed? Which have been the most difficult?

Describe your school. Are learning and academic success respected? Has your school encouraged you to develop your interests, talents, and abilities? Have you felt pressured by academic demands? What would you change and what would you preserve about your school?

Do you enjoy reading? What is the last book you chose to read that was not assigned? Do you have a favorite book or author?

What has been your most stimulating intellectual experience in recent years?

How well has your school prepared you for college? Have you been challenged by your courses? Which ones, in particular?

Is your academic record accurately representative of your abilities? Is your SAT I or ACT?

Are there outside circumstances in your recent experience or in your background that have interfered with your academic performance?

ACTIVITIES AND INTERESTS

What activities do you enjoy the most? Which has had the most significant impact on your growth or thinking?

Do your activities show any pattern of commitment, competence, or contributions?

How would others describe your role in your school or home community? What do you consider your most important contribution?

After a long, hard day, what do you enjoy doing?

THE WORLD AROUND YOU

What will be your generation's biggest challenge?

How would you describe your family or hometown? How has your environment influenced your thinking?

What do your parents expect of you? What standards have you set for yourself?

What has been the most controversial issue in your school recently? Does this issue concern you? What is your opinion about the issue?

Have you encountered people who thought and acted differently than you do? What viewpoints were most unsettling? How did you respond? How did this experience help you to learn more about yourself?

What distresses you most about the world? Where would you like to start to change it?

PERSONALITY AND RELATIONSHIPS

How would someone who knows you well describe you? What are your strengths and limitations? How have you changed during your high school years?

What three adjectives best describe you?

Which relationships are most important to you and why? Describe your best friends. In what ways are they similar to or different from you?

Describe the groups in your school. To which do you belong? Are you someone who bridges different social groups?

How have others influenced you? What pressures have you felt to conform? How do you respond to peer and academic pressure? How do you react to criticism or failure?

What is the best or most important decision you have made lately?

Would you describe yourself as a risk-taker? Give an example.

Do you enjoy being thrust into new situations with new people, or do you prefer the familiar? How easily do you adjust to new situations?

WHIMSICAL QUESTIONS

If you were not a human, what animal would you like to be?

How would you like to be remembered?

What are you doing ten years from now?

What is your favorite: song, color, film, magazine, time of day, word or expression?

What questions do you have for the interview?

While prospective employers might ask some of the some questions above, in addition they might include:

Give an example of working as part of a group or team toward a common goal.

Have you faced an ethical dilemma? If so, how did you resolve it?

Share an experience where you dealt with failure or disappointment. What have you learned from it?

What interests you about this company? What role do you envision for yourself in it?

What skills of yours do you think will be most useful for your work here?

What are your long-range goals? What do you hope to learn here?

Sample Student Résumé

NAME

Home Address   School Class of
Phone Number   School Address
E-mail   Phone Number

EXTRACURRICULAR ACTIVITIES

School Organizations and Clubs

Yearbook, Editorial Staff, 11th   4 hrs/wk, 40 wks/yr
and 12th

Model UN, Member, 10th, 11th,   1 hr/wk, 20 wks/yr
and 12th

COMMUNITY SERVICE

DOROT, Volunteer   1 hr/wk, 15 wks/yr

Delivered meals to homebound
elderly people

ATHLETICS

Varsity Soccer, Captain 12th,   15 hrs/wk, 8 wks/yr
Center Midfield, 9th–12th   First   Outstanding
                                 Player Award, 9th

INTERNSHIPS AND EMPLOYMENT

Rockefeller University, Research   2 hrs/wk, 20 wks/yr
Intern, 11th and 12th

Assisted university professor in Genome research for
article to be published in professional journal with
credit to my name as member of the team

The Gap, Stockperson 11th   Summer 2007

SUMMER EXPERIENCE

Language and Learning and   4 wks/July '06
Travel Program-France 10th

Seacrest   Tennis   Academy,   2 wks/June '05
Tampa, Florida

Extended Biographies

Frank C. Leana has worked with students, families, and schools for over thirty-five years. In 2001, he founded Frank C. Leana, PhD, Educational Counseling in New York City.

Dr. Leana received his AB with Honors from Hamilton College, his MA from Indiana University, and a doctorate in English from the University of Rochester. He earned a Certificate from Harvard University Graduate School of Counseling Institute.

Dr. Leana is the author of *Getting into College,* published by Noonday Press and *The Best Private Schools and How to Get In,* published by Princeton Review/Random House. He has been cited in *New York* magazine's "Best of New York" and by the *New York Times* as "one of the city's prominent college counselors."

Carole S. Clark conducted research and interviewed as an executive recruiter. Other prior experience includes parent/alumni/development work at the Trinity School in Manhattan.

Ms. Clark graduated with a BA in psychology from Hunter College, holds an MEd from Queens College, and has done postgraduate study in educational counseling at Hunter College. With Dr. Leana she is coauthor of the article "Can You Get Us into Harvard?" published in *College Bound,* March 2005.